CRAFT IT!

Holiday

Gifts

Anastasia Suen

Rourke
Educational Media

rourkeeducationalmedia.com

TABLE OF CONTENTS

Materials Needed for All Projects 4

Holiday Gifts 6

Styrofoam Print Cards 7

Tiny Treasures 11

Silver Snowflake Frames 15

Stamped Clay 19

No-Sew Scarf 23

Winter Flowers 27

Glossary 30

Index 31

Show What You Know 31

Websites to Visit 31

About the Author 32

MATERIALS NEEDED FOR ALL PROJECTS

- air-dry clay
- ballpoint pen
- cookie cutters
- cookie or candy tin
- cord or ribbon
- decoupage
- drinking straw
- fleece
- gift tag
- glass jars
- glitter glaze
- glitter glue
- glue
- hole punch
- masking tape
- measuring tape or ruler
- newspaper or cloth to cover your work area
- paint (various colors)
- paintbrushes (various sizes)
- paint roller
- paint tray
- paper
- paper plates
- Paperwhite Narcissus bulbs
- pebbles
- pencil
- picture frame
- rolling pin
- scissors

- silver spray paint
- stamps
- stickers
- Styrofoam plates or trays
- spoon
- wax paper

HOLIDAY GIFTS

The winter holidays are here! It is the season for giving. Print your own holiday cards. Decorate a tiny tin to fill with treasures. Make silver snowflakes and golden ornaments. Share a winter flower. Cut and tie a no-sew scarf. Show your love with a handmade gift.

TIP!

Make a holiday gift that can be used year after year.

Print your own holiday cards!

Here's How:

1. Fold colorful paper in half to make your cards.
2. Cut out a square of a different color paper, slightly smaller than the folded cards.

You Will Need:
- newspaper or cloth to cover your work area
- ballpoint pen
- Styrofoam plates or washed and dried food trays
- scissors
- ruler
- paper plate or paint tray
- paint
- paint roller
- spoon
- paper for printing
- glue

3. Cut out a four by four inch (10.16 centimeter by 10.16 centimeter) square of Styrofoam.

4. Draw a picture in the center of the square. Use a ballpoint pen.

5. Squeeze paint onto a plate or paint tray.

6. Roll it out. Cover the entire roller with paint.

7. Roll the paint on your picture.

8. Cover the entire square with paint.

TIP!

Press the pen hard enough to make a mark but not a hole.

9. Carefully place the front of the smaller paper on the paint.

10. Rub the back of the paper with a spoon. That will help the paint stick evenly.

11. Slowly peel the paper off. Turn it over to dry.

12. Glue the printed paper onto your folded card.

TIP!

The print will be a mirror image of your design.

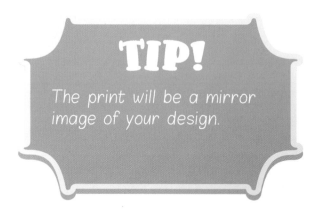

Decorate a tiny tin to fill with small treasures.

Here's How:

1. Wash and dry a small cookie or candy tin.
2. Turn the tin upside down on a sheet of colorful paper.
3. Trace a line around the lid. Cut out the shape.

TIP!

Cut the paper just inside the pencil line, so you won't have to erase it later.

4. Brush glue or **decoupage** on the top of the tin.
5. Place the paper on the glue. Smooth out the bubbles with your finger.
6. Brush glue or decoupage over the top of the paper. Let it dry overnight.

7. Decorate the lid. Use paper, ribbons, or stickers.
8. Measure and cut. Glue on one item at a time.
9. Dry the tin overnight.

TIP!
After the top dries, open the tin and scrape off any extra glue. If there is glue on the edges or the **hinges**, the tin won't open properly.

10. Fill the tin with small treasures.

You Will Need:
- newspaper or cloth to cover your work area
- picture frame
- silver spray paint
- pencil
- paper
- glitter glue
- wax paper
- glue

Add glitter snowflakes to a picture frame.

Here's How:

1. Remove the back, paper insert, and glass from the picture frame.

2. Go outside. Spray the frame silver. Ask an adult to help you.

TIP!

Breathing paint fumes is dangerous. Only spray paint outside in a well-ventilated area.

3. Draw small snowflakes on paper.

4. Place wax paper over your drawings.

5. Trace the snowflakes with glitter glue.

6. Let the glitter glue dry overnight.

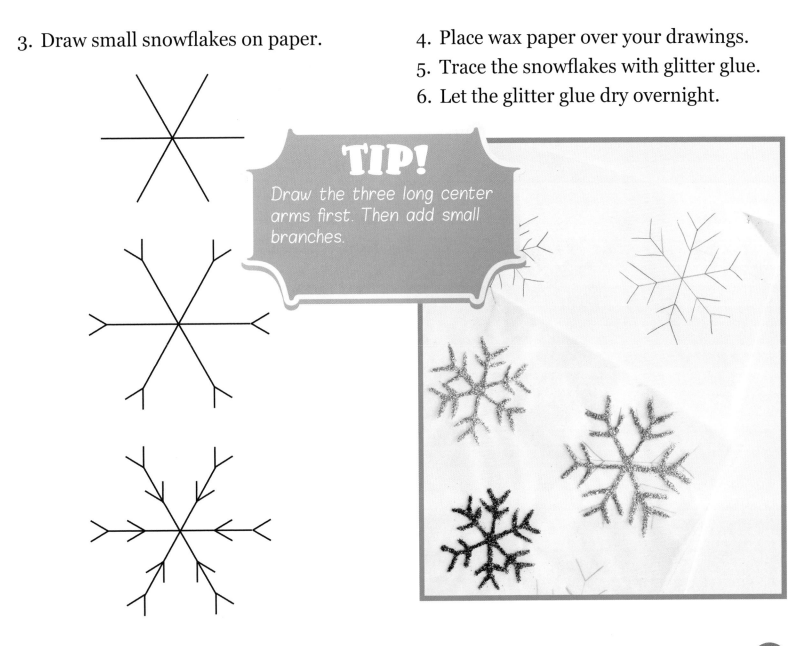

TIP!

Draw the three long center arms first. Then add small branches.

7. Gently peel the snowflakes off the waxed paper.
8. Place glue on the picture frame.
9. Glue down one snowflake at a time.

Make a snowy scene.

If you make large snowflakes, you can glue them inside a frame instead. Measure and cut blue paper to fit inside the frame. Draw snowflakes on the blue paper and trace them with glitter glue. The next day, carefully place the blue paper inside the frame and close the back. Do not add the glass.

Hang these stamped clay ornaments on a tree. Or use them as gift tags.

Here's How:

1. Roll the clay in your hands to warm it up.
2. Roll it out flat on a clean surface.
3. Press a cookie cutter into the clay.
4. Lift up the cookie cutter and remove the shape.

TIP!

If the clay is too bumpy, use a rolling pin to make it flat.

5. Stamp a design onto the clay.

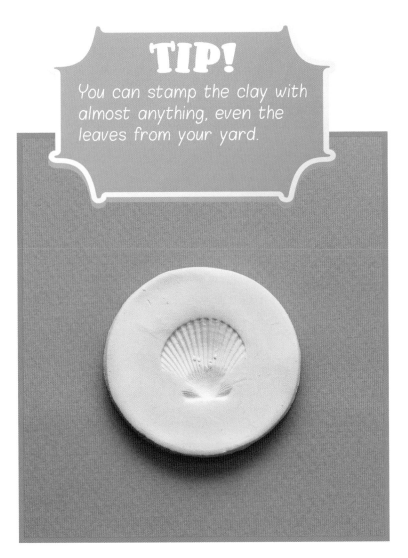

TIP!

You can stamp the clay with almost anything, even the leaves from your yard.

6. Press a drinking straw into the clay to make a hole.

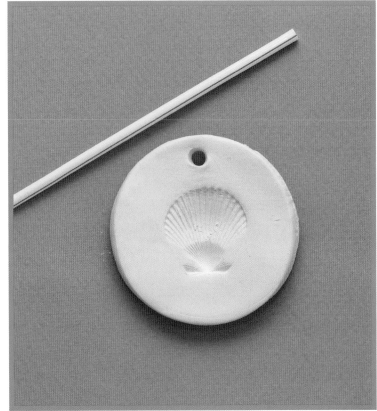

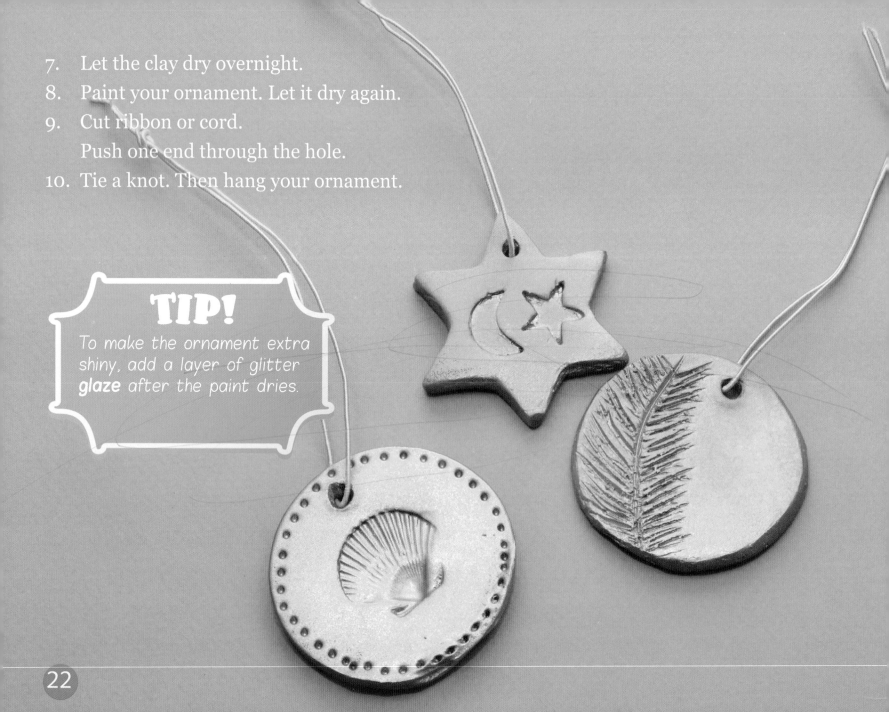

7. Let the clay dry overnight.
8. Paint your ornament. Let it dry again.
9. Cut ribbon or cord.
   Push one end through the hole.
10. Tie a knot. Then hang your ornament.

TIP!

To make the ornament extra shiny, add a layer of glitter *glaze* after the paint dries.

You Will Need:
- fleece (one quarter yard or 23 centimeters)
- measuring tape or ruler
- scissors
- masking tape

Make a warm scarf in minutes.

Here's How:

1. Clean up the edge of the fleece. Cut off the **selvedge**.

TIP!

The selvedge is the edge of a bolt of cloth. Some fabric companies use it like a label and write the product information there.

2. Place masking tape three inches (7.6 centimeters) from each end.
3. Place the measuring tape above the masking tape. Mark the tape at each inch (2.54 centimeters).
4. Cut from the edge of the cloth to the marks on the tape.

5. Cut **fringe** on each end of the scarf.
6. Remove the masking tape. Tie a knot at the top of each strand of fringe.

TIP!

For longer fringe, place the tape four inches (10 centimeters) from the edge.

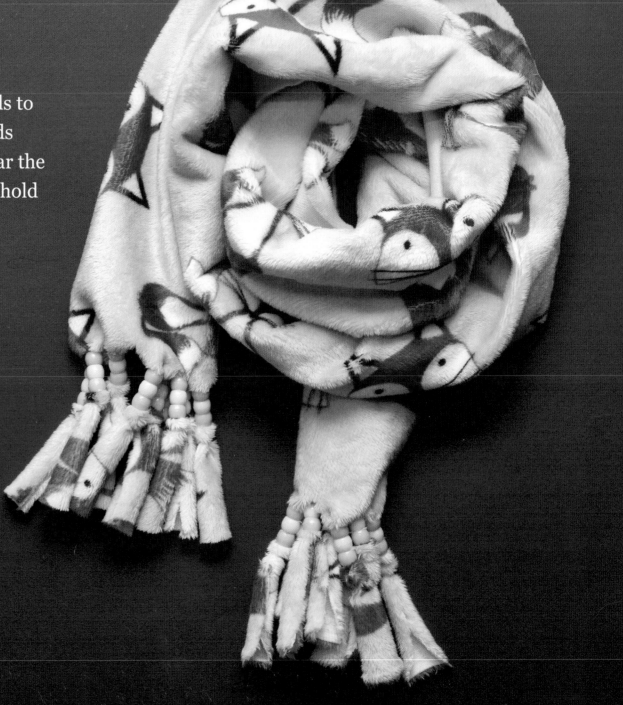

Add Beads!

If you want to add beads to the fringe, add the beads first, then tie a knot near the bottom of the fringe to hold the beads in place.

Give a winter flower.

Here's How:

1. Open a glass jar.
2. Place small pebbles in the jar.
3. Place a flower **bulb** on top of the pebbles.

4. Add water to the rocks under the bulb. Do not get the bulb wet.
5. Tie the ribbon around the jar. Make a bow.

TIP!

Attach a gift tag with a note:

"I am a Paperwhite Narcissus bulb. Keep my roots covered with water so I can grow. I will flower in two to three weeks."

GLOSSARY

bulb (BUHLB): the underground part of a plant that grows buds on top and roots below

decoupage (day-koo-PAHZH): glue used to hold and seal cut paper to another item

fringe (FRINJ): a decorative border of hanging strips or threads

glaze (GLAYZ): a coat of liquid that adds a shiny finish

hinges (HINJSS): movable metal joints on a lid or a door

selvedge (SEL-vij): the edge of a bolt of cloth

INDEX

bulb 28, 29

card(s) 6, 7, 8, 10

clay 19, 20, 21, 22

flower(s) 6, 27, 28, 29

frame(s) 15, 16, 18

glue 8, 10, 12, 13, 16, 17, 18

jar 28, 29

ornament(s) 6, 20, 22

paint 8, 9, 10, 16, 20, 22

scarf 6, 23, 24, 25

snowflakes 6, 16, 17, 18

Styrofoam 7, 8, 9

tin 6, 12, 13, 14

SHOW WHAT YOU KNOW

1. Why is a spoon used to make prints?

2. Explain why extra glue must be scraped off the tin each time.

3. What can you use to stamp a clay ornament?

4. Explain where and why knots are tied in the fringe of a scarf.

5. What will grow into the rocks in the jar?

WEBSITES TO VISIT

http://crafts.lovetoknow.com/wiki/Decoupage_for_Kids

www.kinderart.com/printmaking/print102.shtml

www.cremedelacraft.com/2012/05/diy-no-sew-tote-bag-from-pillow-case.html

ABOUT THE AUTHOR

As a child, Anastasia Suen made her first winter holiday cards and gifts at the kitchen table. Today she uses the same kitchen table to make holiday cards and gifts in her studio in Northern California.

Meet The Author!
www.meetREMauthors.com

www.rourkeeducationalmedia.com

PHOTO CREDITS: All photos © Blue Door Publishing, FL except the following from Shutterstock.com: tip box throughout © caesart; pages 4-5 © FabrikaSimf; page 6 © Inha Makeyeva; page 15 background photo without snowflake frame © Africa Studio; photo of snowman © Giorgiolo; page 18 silver frame on right without snowflakes © ZynatiszJay; page 27 background photo without jar and flowers © S_Photo, flowers © Sergieiev page 30 © Tumana

Edited by: Keli Sipperley

Cover and Interior design by: Nicola Stratford   www.nicolastratford.com
Thank you, Ashley Hayasaka, for making the crafts.

Library of Congress PCN Data

Holiday Gifts / Anastasia Suen
(Craft It!)
 ISBN 978-1-68342-376-8 (hard cover)
 ISBN 978-1-68342-885-5 (soft cover)
 ISBN 978-1-68342-542-7 (e-Book)
Library of Congress Control Number: 2017931276

Rourke Educational Media
Printed in the United States of America, North Mankato, Minnesota